Lancaster County: A Keepsake

A Keepsake

LANCASTER COUNTY

Don Shenk

SCHIFFER
PUBLISHING

4880 Lower Valley Road • Atglen, PA 19310

Published by Schiffer Publishing, Ltd.
4880 Lower Valley Road
Atglen, PA 19310
Phone: (610) 593-1777; Fax: (610) 593-2002
E-mail: Info@schifferbooks.com
Web: www.schifferbooks.com

For our complete selection of fine books on this and related
subjects, please visit our website at www.schifferbooks.com.
You may also write for a free catalog.

Schiffer Publishing's titles are available at special discounts
for bulk purchases for sales promotions or premiums.
Special editions, including personalized covers, corporate
imprints, and excerpts, can be created in large quantities for
special needs. For more information, contact the publisher.

We are always looking for people to write books on new and
related subjects. If you have an idea for a book, please
contact us at proposals@schifferbooks.com.

INTRODUCTION

Lancaster County is located in south-central Pennsylvania and has been referred to as "the Garden Spot of America." That is because it has the most fertile nonirrigated soil in the United States and produces nearly 20 percent of the state's agricultural output. Tourism has become a large industry in Lancaster County, much of the interest being the largest, best-known, and most-visited Amish settlement in the world. Other highlights include its covered bridges, the revitalized city of Lancaster, many historical sites, and picturesque farms and small towns located throughout the county.

Amish boy at Mud Sale

Amish lads at Mud Sale

Playing at a horse auction

Horse auction

Steam tractor exits field

Planting vegetables

Planting peach trees

Apple blossoms

Cherry blossoms

Quince blossoms

Artist in peach orchard

Working in apple orchard

Pollinators in orchard

Purple weed

Tug of war

Planting tobacco

Planting tobacco

Kayaking on Pequea Creek

Cutting grain

Children in a grain field

Loading grain

Threshing grain

Baling straw

Selling produce at Central Market

Vegetables at Central Market

Sunflower

Scooters at an Amish school

Pony cart ride

Children peering from porch

Covered bridge

Chopping hay

Free-range chickens

Leaving a church service

Picturesque farm

Traveling along a country road

Spring day at the farm

Farm in southern Lancaster County

Amish farm

Roadside produce stand

Going to hayfield through cornfield

Harvesting corn

Great day to go fishing

Horse in shed

Windmill

Country lane

Amish farm

Cows at country fair

Petting cow at fair

Strasburg Rail Road

Hayride to pumpkin patch

Pumpkins

Picking corn

Scenic farms

Amish boys with ear of corn

Amish children with pony

Beautiful farm

Scenic fall day

Corn harvest

Covered bridge

Peaceful fall day

Gorgeous autumn day

Cows on autumn day

Octoraro Lake

Through the woods

Fishing Creek Nature Preserve

Southern Lancaster County farm in autumn

Pinnacle Point

Northeastern Lancaster County farm

Northern Lancaster County farm

Sunday afternoon ride

Gorgeous fall day

Ready for harvest

Awe-inspiring fall day

Central Manor Church

Hans Herr House

Farm observation silo

Alpaca

Sheep

Tractor

Steam and cinders

Snowy day

Horse barn

Wonderful winter day

Buggies

Cold winter day

Sleigh ride

Covered bridge

Covered bridge

Spring snow

Scooters